HUMMINGBIRDS

HUMMINGBIRDS

PETER MURRAY
THE CHILD'S WORLD

You hear it before you see it: a strange noise, a sort of buzzing sound. *BZZZZZZ!* Is it a giant bee? No, it's more like a humming sound. *MMMMMM!* There it is, a bright green blur. It stops in your garden, hovering in midair, sparkling red, green, and blue. It dips its long, pointed beak into a bright red flower. *MMMZZZP!* It's gone! A hummingbird!

When a hummingbird drops in for a visit, it does not stay in one place for long. This busy little bird zips from flower to flower, licking the sweet nectar from each bright blossom. When sunlight hits these colorful birds just right, you can see why people call them "feathered jewels." Hummingbirds use up a lot of energy, so they need lots of food. Before you know it, this one's off to check out your neighbor's flowers. *MMMZZZP!*

Hummingbirds are found only in the Americas. Most of them live in the warm regions of South and Central America. During the summer, however, hummingbirds migrate to wherever wildflowers bloom. The *ruby-throated hummingbird* flies 500 miles nonstop across the Gulf of Mexico. The tiny *rufous hummingbird*, shown in this photograph, migrates between Central America and Alaska. It travels 2,500 miles every spring and fall! During their migration, hummingbirds live on fat reserves stored in their bodies.

Because they are so active, hummingbirds must spend much of their time eating. Their favorite food is the sweet, energy-rich nectar of flowers. Flower nectar supplies hummingbirds with water, sugar, vitamins, and minerals.

Hummingbirds seem to prefer red flowers, but any color will do. One bird might visit 1,000 flowers a day! It pushes its beak deep into the flower and laps up the nectar with its long tongue.

Many flowers rely on hummingbirds to help them reproduce. When a hummingbird feeds, pollen from the flower sticks to its beak. Later, as the bird visits the next flower, a few grains of pollen rub off. This transfer of pollen from one flower to another is called *pollination*. Without pollination, a flower's seeds cannot grow. The hummingbird helps itself to each flower's nectar and, at the same time, helps the flower make seeds—a good deal for everybody involved!

Nectar supplies most of the hummingbird's food, but not all of it. Ruby-throated hummingbirds sometimes sip tree sap from woodpecker holes. In early spring, before wildflowers bloom, the birds follow woodpeckers from tree to tree, hoping for a meal.

Hummingbirds also eat insects they find in flowers. Sometimes a hummingbird steals an insect from a spider web, or grabs one right out of the air! The young ruby-throat in this photograph is not quite big enough to eat this butterfly. It will have to wait its turn for a sip of flower nectar.

A hummingbird's magical, darting flight is wonderful to watch. This little acrobat can stop in midair, sip a little nectar, then take off—*ZZZZZZZP!*—so fast you aren't even sure which way it went. As if turbo-powered, these birds can go from a complete stop to full speed in less than a second. And you never know which way a hummingbird is going to fly. Like tiny feathered helicopters, hummingbirds can fly straight up, down, forward, or backward. They can even fly upside down!

A full-grown hummingbird weighs less than a pencil, but its tiny size doesn't stop it from defending its territory! Hummingbirds fearlessly attack big birds such as crows, blue jays, and even hawks. Ounce for ounce, the hummingbird is one of the toughest birds in the garden.

During breeding season, male hummingbirds sometimes fight with each other over the females. They attack with their claws and sharp beaks. Imagine how big that 2-inch-long beak looks to a 3½-inch-long hummingbird!

Male hummingbirds are more brightly colored than females. Their bright feathers help attract potential mates. When a male hummingbird finds a female, he puts on a show to impress her. Flying high into the air, he shrieks and dives straight down in front of the female. Just when it looks like he's going to hit the ground, he pulls up, looping, swooping, and showing off his bright colors. This is called an *aerial display*. If the female likes the show, the two birds mate.

After mating, the female hummingbird weaves pine needles, dried flowers, moss, grasses, and bits of lichen into a tiny nest. She uses sticky spider webs to hold it all together. Her whole nest is little bigger than a walnut! The outside of the nest is hard, tough, and waterproof. The inside, cushioned with a layer of cobwebs and feathers, is soft and cozy.

Once she finishes building her nest, the hummingbird lays two white eggs, each about the size of a navy bean. The eggs hatch in about two weeks.

When they first hatch, baby hummingbirds are blind and featherless, but they soon open their eyes and grow feathers. The babies are very hungry right from the start. Feeding her babies keeps the mother hummingbird constantly busy. She stores insects and flower nectar inside her body, then pushes her beak deep into the babies' throats and pumps the food into them.

The babies grow quickly. Within three weeks they climb onto the edge of the nest and take flight! The young hummingbirds stay with their mother for a few more weeks, until they learn to find their own food.

Hummingbirds are such quick, agile flyers, even when young, that they can escape from most predators. However, they must always be on the lookout for danger. Hawks, cats, bullfrogs, and snakes all eat hummingbirds—if they can catch them.

One of the greatest dangers to hummingbirds is cold weather. If the temperature gets too cold, a hummingbird fluffs up its feathers and goes into a deep sleep called *torpor*. During torpor, the bird's heart rate and breathing slows down and its body temperature drops. When the weather warms, the hummingbird wakes up and goes about its business.

Have you seen hummingbirds near your home? If not, you can attract them by planting lots of bright red flowers. Hummingbirds like columbine, petunias, hollyhocks, and many other easy-to-grow flowers. You can also put up a hummingbird feeder and fill it with artificial nectar. Sooner or later, the hummingbirds will come. You might get a whole flock of them zooming and zipping around. Did you hear something? *MMMZZZP!* There it is!

INDEX

PHOTO RESEARCH

Charles Rotter/Archipelago Productions

PHOTO CREDITS

J. H. Robinson: front cover, 7, 13, 14, 18, 22

Joe McDonald: 2, 4, 21, 28, 31

COMSTOCK/George Lepp: 8, 17, 24

Len Rue, Jr.: 11

Leonard Rue III: 27

Library of Congress Cataloging-in-Publication Data
Murray, Peter, 1952 Sept. 29-
Hummingbirds / by Peter Murray.
p. cm.
Summary: Describes the physical characteristics,
habits, and behavior of hummingbirds.
ISBN 1-56766-011-9
1. Hummingbirds--Juvenile literature.
[1. Hummingbirds.]   I. Title.
QL696.A558M87   1993   92-32320
598'.899--dc20   CIP
                                        AC

Distributed to schools and libraries in the United States by
ENCYCLOPAEDIA BRITANNICA EDUCATIONAL CORP.
310 South Michigan Avenue
Chicago, Illinois 60604